In Days to Come

BY "ASHTAR"

*Received through Automatic Writing
by Ethel P. Hill*

VOL. I

First published in 1957

Published by Left of Brain Books

Copyright © 2023 Left of Brain Books

ISBN 978-1-396-32482-6

First Edition

All rights reserved. No part of this publication may be reproduced, distributed, or transmitted in any form or by any means, including photocopying, recording, or other electronic or mechanical methods, without the prior written permission of the publisher, except in the case of brief quotations permitted by copyright law. Left of Brain Books is a division of Left Of Brain Onboarding Pty Ltd.

PUBLISHER'S PREFACE

About the Book

"This is a series of messages from an extraterrestrial entity named Ashtar, purportedly transmitted via 'automatic writing.' Ashtar was apparently channeled by Ethel P. Hill, an early UFO contactee. Ashtar claims to be the commander of a vast army of spacemen. He apparently reports directly to Jesus Christ, who, it is implied, will return at some point in a UFO.

Ashtar is a desultory speller, and sometimes slips into a bogus King James Bible-style English. One giveaway is his use of the word 'thyselves,' a neologism based on 'thyself.' The correct form of the second person plural possessive has been 'yourselves' since Old English.

Ashtar's message is both reassuring and vaguely terrifying. His constant reassurances that he has come (or will come, 'real soon now') to fix our problems, not to conquer, only deepen the concern. So, hedging my bets, just in case Ashtar is listening out there, let me be the first to welcome Earth's new alien overlords"

(Quote from sacred-texts.com)

CONTENTS

PUBLISHER'S PREFACE
FOREWORD 1
INTRODUCTION 10
    CHAPTER I. 13
    CHAPTER II. 16
    CHAPTER III. 19
    CHAPTER IV. 22
    CHAPTER V. 25
    CHAPTER VI. 29
    CHAPTER VII. 33
    CHAPTER VII. 38
    CHAPTER IX 41
    CHAPTER X. 46
    CHAPTER XI. 49
    CHAPTER XII. 52
    CHAPTER XIII. 55
    CHAPTER XIV. 59
    CHAPTER XV. 64

FOREWORD

AS spiritual pioneers of the New Age, there are many things to consider. Certainly the coming of the so-called Flying Saucers is a momentous "sign of the times," and the attitude taken towards them is an unmistakable measuring rod of your intelligence and spiritual status.

People interested in Flying Saucers fall into three categories— those who are indifferent to the whole matter, those who are interested only in the physical aspects, who pride themselves on their "scientific attitude," but close their mind to every evidence not in keeping with their own theories, and those who "believe" in Flying Saucers and the possibility of communication with Spacemen.

Among the latter we find some, it is true, who are mentally not capable of weighing evidence and the nature of various reports and "believe" everybody who claims to have made a contact with Spacemen and every wild story. Naturally such people are ridiculed by the more "sober minded," who reserve judgment until they find some evidence for acceptance. On the other hand, is he who senses the tremendous import of Flying Saucers any less intelligent than he who point blank refuses to even *consider* the possibility of higher worlds and communications with Spacemen through extrasensory perception?

Extrasensory perception is now scientifically proven, established by Prof. Rhine of Duke University. And why shouldn't' beings from Outer Space, more advanced in this sort of thing, communicate with receptive individuals here on earth?

Now, a high degree of development of both intelligence and extrasensory perception is of course, ideal, but the lack of the former is no more regrettable than the lack of the latter. As to "men of science," they must necessarily have highly trained minds, but they may be utterly lacking in extrasensory perception or any sort of spiritual perception, which requires the unfoldment of latent, little known faculties in man.

Fortunately for humanity, the number of those who intuitively feel the possibility of intercommunication between dwellers on this planet and in other worlds, is constantly growing and the biting ridicule of materialists cannot shake their faith, for the earth is moving into a new "dimension" and the requirements for the "survival of the fittest" is changing. Once it was brawn, but now it is precisely the extrasensory faculty. The life of many a soldier has been saved by a sudden "hunch." Mental telepathy will be far more common in the future and one day will be considered "standard equipment." For the present, the man or woman who has it, is far more likely to survive in these days of earthquakes, floods and bombings.

For he or she who gets the "hunch" to leave a certain place *before* a bomb falls, before an earthquake rocks the house, or fire breaks out, has a far greater chance to survive than those who do not have such "hunches." A man may be smart enough to "get the best of the other fellow," strong as an ox, and very "practical," and have a well trained mind, but still may not be able to foresee disaster.

In these perilous times, it is not necessarily the one with the biggest bank roll, or who is socially secure, and has a private bomb shelter, who will survive, but rather the one who has learned to follow hunches, who feels an inner "guidance," and remains calm.

In a recent lecture Franklin Thomas pointed out that in the New Age, thoughts will be increasingly visible, and therefore deception and what is now called "hypocrisy" will be of no avail. For the present, a man or woman, who can sense the motive or feel the thoughts of another, is certainly in a much "safer" position than one who is easily fooled by a charming personality or by first class "acting." I know a man who can lie with complete assurance, look you straight in the eye, while recounting the most fantastic lies, and he fools many so-called "intelligent" people. Whole fortunes and certainly lives have been lost or ruined because someone "trusted" the wrong person.

So . . . the possession of extrasensory perception is no longer a faculty that can be considered a rare luxury, but rather a *necessity for survival*. In the Bible we are told that in the last days even the elect would be deceived, *if* it were possible . . . Evil loves to hide itself under many different kinds of cloaks, and the most dangerous enemy is one who is skilled in perfect deception.

Now, as to extrasensory perception in connection with communication with higher worlds and beings—this is, of course, the first requirement in such a relationship. A person, no matter how much and how often he may "affirm" his divine perfection, if he isn't *receptive* and sensitive to higher influences, will not and cannot receive any instruction from higher sources. It takes a humble and receptive mind, well disciplined and properly "attuned." And before any attempt be made to commune with higher beings, let it be said that one should first learn how to get in touch with one's own higher self, sometimes called the "guardian angel."

Now here we come to an important point. Modern metaphysics, although it has helped thousands, made them more self-reliant, positive in their thinking, intellectually mature and responsible, nevertheless has practically ignored the fact that there are beings in this universe beside ourselves, beings which the ancients sometimes called angels, and who are now being called "space men."

According to occult science and the Bible, there are orders of beings, called by various names, who in times of great need, especially, come to earth to offer their assistance to men. Why shouldn't they be able to impress thoughts and ideas on receptive individuals?

All down the ages there have been mystics who claimed to have heard the VOICE OF GOD or of angels. Today there are those who claim to hear the voice of spacemen. And if Flying Saucers are real—and the Air Force knows they are—why shouldn't they be "manned" by intelligent beings who can send their thought-waves to those who are receptive?

Of course, that doesn't mean that everyone who claims to have received a message has a genuine one from a Spaceman. We are not discussing spiritualism, as such, in the sense of getting messages from one's departed relatives. We are here only considering the possibility of communicating with beings from another world, who come here on a "mission." Perchance they once were incarnate here on earth and therefore have our interest at heart. Perhaps they never were human in our sense of the word, but who nevertheless have intelligence, insight into our problems and understanding of our needs.

Some say that Jesus came here from another planet. Why not? The interest in Flying Saucers is raising many questions. Perhaps there are beings on other planets that never made such a mess of things as we have done here on earth.

According to Jacob Lorber, there are beings who did not "fall" and forget their divine origin, but remained in their *pristine* purity. Perhaps most of us here are "prodigal sons." There are said to be men and women who have lived on other planets, and are here on earth to learn certain lessons which can only be learned on earth—through a temporary forgetfulness of their inner divinity and by working upward through the darkness, step by step. Perhaps there are those who are only here to help and instruct us.

At any rate, our earth is certainly not the only inhabited planet in this vast universe. And one thing is sure, we have made a mess of our affairs, and we are in sore need of help and guidance from higher powers at this particular time.

Now, some say that any kind of spirit communication is evil. Some claim that, according to the Bible, it is wicked to call back the dead but the Bible itself is full of communications with spirits of departed ones. Even Jesus spoke to Elijah and Moses on the Mount of Transfiguration. But of course, just about anything can be proven or disproven by Bible texts. The Bible is written in such a way that there can be many interpretations depending on your understanding. Often, passages are interpreted according to wishful thinking or the misunderstanding of ancient symbolism. As to metaphysical teachers, who usually ignore the possibility of spirit communication, most leaders themselves, even Mrs. Eddy (who so violently opposed it), have been known to commune with departed ones.

Now, the communion with higher beings can take place in various ways, one of which is automatic writing, where the hand writes without being directed by the conscious mind of the medium, or by mental telepathy, or the hearing of an inner voice. Automatic writing depends, of course, on the willingness of the individual to be a channel of communication and to what extent the conscious mind is temporarily put in abeyance.

Regarding the communication from Ashtar, received through automatic writing by E. P. H. (who prefers to remain anonymous) there are certain interesting side lights. Here is the story:

We had been receiving the Ashtar discourses from E. P. H. at various intervals and considered them of a very high order. Some of them were read on several occasions before our group, but we did not think of spreading the news any further. One morning the thought struck us that we should give the ASHTAR messages wider circulation than was possible through the efforts of E. P. H., who is doing her best to send them to as many people as possible.

That very same day, a friend came to our office and said that the latest communication from this source indicated the expressed wish of ASHTAR that his messages should receive wider circulation. After this "coincidence" we wrote to E. P. H. and told her of our intentions. She not only heartily approved, but received a message from ASHTAR addressed to us at the NEW AGE PUBLISHING CO., expressing a "most hearty approval."

The communication to us says in part: "A service of immeasurable worth has been rendered us in the publishing and circulation of what you call "the Saucer Books." Their influence and the interest they have aroused spreads with ever increasing momentum far beyond your cognizance. We must keep the fountain flowing, with as little contamination as possible from spurious sources." There is also an intimation that messages from Ashtar may come through various *other* "suitable channels."

Since the appearance of the first ASHTAR messages much has transpired. Groups in many cities have formed for the purpose of studying his communications. New channels have also been called to our attention. Although Harold W. Wilkins, author of FLYING SAUCERS UNCENSORED is most critical and highly skeptical of "communications with space beings," nevertheless he gives one ASHTAR message in his book, leaving it to the reader to decide what he or she thinks about it. The contents of the message is of the same high order as the ones contained in this book, which has changed many a life from fear and uncertainty to confidence in the creator and the future.

It is impossible, of course, to check on the source of the material given in the following pages. Error is always possible where extrasensory perception is concerned. However, we offer these discourses to the public for their perusal as we received them—unaltered—and leave it to you to judge as to their value.

Whether Flying Saucers are "air sylphs," as sometimes claimed by some theosophists and other clairvoyants; physical objects, as claimed by Major Donald Keyhoe; Etherships, as suggested by Meade Layne and others, or whether space beings are entities who have once lived on this earth and since resided on other planets, or remained cruising in space, as Daniel Fry points out in THE WHITE SANDS INCIDENT, one thing is certain, Flying Saucers are here and communications with space beings and extra-terrestrials is an interesting phenomena of our times.

The messages received from extra terrestrial source seem to have one thing in common, regardless of where they are received or through what instrumentality. They all, without exception, warn of impending disaster if mankind does not adopt a more tolerant and understanding attitude among nations and peoples, and cease the hydrogen bomb and armament race. Typical of this is the Martian's message to Mr. Von Cihlar in the Austrian mountains, which is quoted in full in "We Come in Peace" by Franklin Thomas.

One more thing, however, should not be neglected at this point: There are many who come to us or write to us, asking us how they may perhaps make a mental contact with beings from Outer Space. Many have on their own started to experiment with the Ouija board. We do not advise this. People who are not properly trained and have no knowledge of spirit communication or the vagaries of the sub-conscious mind, can get into serious trouble playing around with things they do not understand. If any space being or other high intelligence sees that you are ready to become a channel of communication, they will of their own initiative open the way. On your part for the present, it is sufficient that you have high aspirations, a desire to be of service in this great cause and leave the rest to them.

According to the latest communication from ASHTAR, this is his expressed wish. He says, in part, "we, ourselves, will choose the time, place and person we desire to contact. However, it will be of immense assistance if you will maintain a feeling of friendly interest and confidence in us and, in your mind, hold a thought of welcome. Our forces find such an atmosphere well adapted to their work, "as they need these 'lighted landing fields,' where they may pause for a moment or two and adapt themselves to conditions and vibrations they encounter in fulfilling their various assignments."

The path of spiritual unfoldment is a serious one and is beset with many difficulties. First and foremost, discipline is necessary to control the body and mind, without which nothing can be accomplished. The control of thought and feeling before going to sleep is especially important. We cannot go into detail in this short space, but the desire to be of service, and the longing to become a "lighted landing field" is a safe guide in itself. All else will follow. For "when the pupil is ready the Master will appear."

There are many who feel that ASHTAR and his legions are the forerunners of the Second Coming of Christ—no matter how this is understood. Some expect to see him in the flesh, others believe that the Spirit of Christ will eventually rule the earth, and the spiritually "unfit" will be eliminated. At any rate, many people feel that our so-called culture is nearing its end and that something is about to happen. A change must come both in world affairs and in religion whose doctrines were fashioned not by Jesus but by medieval priests in order to keep the ignorant in spiritual bondage to the Church.

The Ancient Wisdom ever remains the same, although Truth may be presented in many forms, and in the course of ages may become covered with the barnacles of superstition.

Great Spiritual Intelligences seek suitable channels to convey spiritual truths, and at times of crisis there is always an influx of "messages" from other worlds.

The Publishers

INTRODUCTION

To Our Friends on the Planet Shan—Greetings!

OUR presence and our purpose grow increasingly clear to all unbiased and unprejudiced people of your earth and thousands eagerly await our visible appearance. While there is ample ground for the belief that we are able to perform what to you appears as miracles, we wish it clearly understood we have nothing in common with charlatans performing legerdemain tricks, either for purposes of entertainment or to "prove" our reality. Every move we make is in pursuance of a well considered plan. I speak for all of us who have embarked upon this somewhat thankless task of rendering assistance to beleaguered dwellers on the planet Shan.

It would be quite a relief if we could make a simultaneous landing on all portions of your globe (which I might remark is entirely feasible at this very moment!) and, employing etheric forces in the use of which we are experts, put an end to the jangle of incongruous and irreconcilable factions now precluding all possibility of a united effort toward peace. Our instructions and our principles prevent our taking such a course.

A predominance of resolution by the inhabitants themselves must precede our entrance on the scene en masse to use our superior powers in augmenting those possessed by mortals at this time. Yes, I most certainly do refer to the H-bomb (and other highly dangerous explosives.) It is one thing to compound and to explode such a hellish contrivance but where is the mortal who has solved the problem of *preventing* its explosion or nullifying its deadly effect? No such person exists on the planet Shan! How dare they release a force of such magnitude without the slightest idea how to control it? None but an infant intellect would conceive of such an insane procedure! Have they seriously considered the resulting phenomena in Nature's vast domain?

Many otherwise intelligent mortals view the eccentricities exhibited by the Nature forces as outside mortal jurisdiction, believing them to be dictated by Divinity Itself! They constantly set waves of destructive thoughts and feeling in motion. Joining like disturbing vibrations, they travel untold distances always creating much havoc in the ethers. Do you suppose these discords, generated by you and millions like you, have no effect on inanimate forces? What you term "disasters" seldom occur on our planets. We have eliminated the causes. When the preponderance of desire and action is heavily weighted in favor of constituents inevitably causing warfare in realms visible or invisible, how may those responsible hope to escape its horrors? If you feel you have escaped this pitfall and promoted peace in every way, I would ask you one question. In your quest for peace (at any price?) have you trodden under foot principles which are indispensable adjuncts of true Peace?

One thing I would make crystal clear! We Space Men, in whatever capacity we may temporarily serve, are irrevocably pledged by the most solemn of oaths to abide by those Universal Laws which alone can preserve life on every level of conscious existence. To accept or condone any variance from these fixed and unchangeable codes governing all honorable behavior, would be to forfeit privileges we have earned through eons of unremitting effort. We will have no part in any form of "synthetic peace!" It must be genuine, unalloyed, incapable of dissimulation.

Before discontinuing I feel impelled to add one word of counsel. Make your own life conform as nearly as possible with the matchless teachings of One who humbled Himself to contact mortals in a physical manifestation. Any likeness to Him will enable us to recognize your legitimate claim to our special attention and assistance.

As future friends and co-workers in the service of your coming King of Kings, we salute you and proffer our utmost devotion in your liberation from all who seek to ensnare you and bind you to their fearsome juggernaut of destructive domination.

WE COME AS YOUR DEFENDERS AND DELIVERERS!

WE COME AT THE URGENT REQUEST OF YOUR HEAVENLY FATHER TO RELEASE YOU FROM INSUFFERABLE BONDAGE. MY LOVE AND MY BLESSINGS!

(Signed) ASHTAR

Commander of ten million Space Men, now occupying bases established within range of your planet..

CHAPTER I.

BEGINNING a series of revelations concerning what is going forward in the activities of those not at this time encased in mortal flesh and those who are, or will be, their associates on the earthplane. Thy friends in the Unseen be possessed of bodies more amenable to transposition from one phase of manifestation to another (as water may manifest as steam, as snow, as ice and so on, depending on atmospheric conditions, natural or artificial.) This doth greatly enhance their ability to aid mortals at this time.

Pardon the diversion! Be ye interested in concrete facts deduced from acute sensitivity to present conditions and their inevitable consequences. As hath been said, the precise moment of Divine Intervention doth depend absolutely upon Man's reaction to tests imposed, not by thy Heavenly Father or His obedient emissaries, but by the dupes of the Enemy.

As ye do at times forget, the warfare doth rage upon the astral planes simultaneously with its progress on the earthplane. The mere fact that so many thousands have been "killed" doth not conclude the matter in any wise. THEY STILL LIVE! Thus our problem is to segregate them, not as to earthly categories but in accord with our innate purposes and desires. Naturally, this doth greatly complicate the task of those whose responsibility it be to resolve the whole matter into its basic constituents.

With regard to thine own country, which be destined to act as a "spring-board" from which to extend *real* aid to other lands, the present distressing exhibition of preposterous antagonism to well-planned, inherently just and legally sanctioned procedures to rid the administrative branches of the government of utterly subversive and traitorous incumbents cannot be tolerated. As dastardly plots of the enemy are exposed to view, it be for the American people to choose whether to cast their lot with the Christ forces or the renegades. There be no middle ground . . . to remain neutral be the most despicable crime of all.

Ye do deplore the lapse of time, yet of what consequence be the amount of time consumed, compared with the self-exposure of criminals posing as benefactors of the human race? Presently many millions of souls will be following a pathway of ever progressive evolution, or doomed to tread the downward path of misery and degradation. Is it not worth the price of a few lagging months of desperate conflict twixt Darkness and Light, twixt vicious Hatred and superhuman Courage to make certain every mortal now living is in his or her rightful place? Not in accord with some arbitrary law or human decision but according to the unerring knowledge and wisdom of Him who doth see and judge the inmost secrets and hidden motives of man's hearts?

I say, it will be settled, not by any natural advantage of superior numbers or the use of weapons devised by scientists who have (or think they have) contacted and harnessed the secret powers of Universal Energy. I SAY, NOT SO! It will be brought to an abrupt and incontrovertible conclusion by "AN ACT OF GOD" comparable to none heretofore known to mortals. This planet be not caught in a net of inextricable difficulties but be emerging from its super-imposed domination by semi-demonic demagogues leading to its destruction. It be placing its trust in the only Power able to deliver it from its impending fate.

I say to thee in all sacred solemnity of pronouncement, THIS THY COUNTRY SHALL BE SAVED AS BY A MIRACLE! I say not it will be a peaceful deliverance but through the unfaltering loyalty of millions who place their faith in thy Master, the Christ of God, this land will be cleansed from the abominations now infesting it. It shall be the center from which shall issue those injunctions and powerful energies which shall lead the world into an intense, burning desire to know and to do the Will of the Lord God of All Creation, as revealed by their coming King, who shall reign over this regenerated world without hindrance from those who now harass and seek to destroy His faithful servants.

CHAPTER II.

BEFORE any appreciable gain can be made by earthly representatives of thy Master's coming kingdom, there must come the downfall of vast numbers of bombastic declaimers of their own inflated belief in their own importance and influence over the people. *Assent gained through fear or force melts to nothingness when assailed by cold logic or intense loyalty to higher concepts!*

A long and arduous warfare hath been waged against "the powers of darkness" impinging upon all earth's inhabitants from invisible citadels where Lucifer long reigned supreme over his vassals (invisible to mortals) assigning them to tasks of fiendish ingenuity to entrap and inveigle human beings into abject slavery to his demands.

By reason of the unremitting diligence of those to whom was relegated the apprehension and elimination of countless millions of demoniacs and demoniacally controlled entities, sworn to obey the edits of their overlord, Lucifer—I say, as a result of this uninterrupted campaign on the astral planes, it now be possible to transfer this battle to the physical plane and repeat the process where mortals may more effectively join in the conflict and observe greater tangible results.

As it doth rage on the physical plane, there be three types of weapons to be employed. First: the actual material armaments necessary for defense purposes. Second: the mental agility to recognize and combat delusive propaganda. Third: the spiritual awareness and moral stamina to move steadily forward, in defiance of all enemy resistance, to establish and maintain a rigorous regime of *honest* government in every phase of human affairs.

Ye may say the present deplorable condition of earthly affairs hath always existed and always will. I SAY NAY! Through man's willful disobedience it hath reached a point where his own most determined efforts to remove the accumulated incubus of overwhelming pressure from subversive forces be well-nigh futile.

Divine intervention (operating through chosen emissaries endowed with power and authority to abolish the hellish system in force when Lucifer and his minions held sway) hath prevailed upon invisible planes adjoining the earth and the roving hordes of diabolical perverters of unresisting mortals be either removed or under control.

Now cometh the final stage in this stupendous project. Not without physical discomfort and suffering may the victory be won. Mortals must prove their mettle. Ye may look upon this time of tribulation as a bitter and unwarranted trespass on thy right to lead a life of honor and dignity. Even so! Yet it doth afford thee a glorious opportunity to show thyselves (sic—JBH) worthy to participate in the responsibilities as well as the privileges of the "Golden Age." Privileges forever denied those now responsible for retarding its inauguration.

No matter how previous be the suffering of many mortals in this final phase in the transformation of thy world, all who will stand firm in their defense of the Right (on whatever battlefield they fight) will soon realize that they have rendered a priceless service to their Master and his conquering legions from outer space, now able to traverse the hitherto impenetrable density of earth's auric envelope and bring succor and strength to the Christ Forces in mortal flesh.

A change cometh swiftly over the face of the earth and the peoples residing thereon. Hour by hour the forces of evil themselves disclose their dire purposes. Close upon the heels of these disclosures come the rapidly maturing decisions of the Enlightened Ones now dwelling in fleshly bodies, to reverse the edicts of false leaders and substitute their own true concepts of constructive action to insure the survival of desperately beleaguered followers of One sent to teach men the Way of Life!

CHAPTER III.

I salute You from Schare! A few further words of explanation regarding our presence and purpose. At the request of your Heavenly Father, we come to assist your Unseen Guardians who are greatly perturbed over the state of your planet Shan. We come ten million strong with a full complement of appliances and all necessary forces of an etheric nature to use in any manner deemed expedient to block the designs of destructive forces or render their weapons innocuous. We realize certain portions of earthly terrain are marked *for* destruction. In pursuance of this program, we withhold interference when so instructed by the Hierarchy in uninterrupted touch with the Father of us all. When certain prearranged signals are received, we send thousands of ventlas to places where dangerous conditions exist.

Perhaps, you will more readily comprehend our mission of merciful protection when I tell you countless instances of planned sabotage have gone awry owing to the vigilance and prompt action of our men. Destruction for destruction's sake is not our practice. A condition may be most distressing and call forth our earnest desire to render assistance, yet we are bound by the most sacred of vows to intervene only at the times and places indicated by our Master or His accredited lieutenants. Once given implicit instructions regarding a particular situation, we are then free to work out the minutiae of operations according to our best wisdom and skill. But there is never a moment when we may not confer with our Commander-in-Chief should we feel any doubt over some proposed step to be taken.

Our means of thought communication and visual observation of any person or place on the entire globe is beyond your present comprehension. It makes possible the fulfilling of a promise many times repeated, that all who put their trust in God will be Divinely protected under all circumstances. Your Heavenly Father uses His dedicated servants to carry out His will, choosing the ones best fitted to act in the various roles demanded in any crisis.

Our appearance in physical form or the materializing of the ships we use occur only on instructions from our Headquarters far above your bases in your stratosphere. They follow a predetermined schedule, not as your clocks and calendars but in conformity with carefully computed sequences of events depending largely on mortal reactions to each step in the program. Many factors enter into the decisions made, such as planetary influences of a magnetic type, astral conditions, the activity of forces concealed within the earth body, constantly changing vibratory rates in different sections of the globe owing to the people's awakening to their perils and desperate attempts to extricate themselves. This latter consideration is perhaps the most potent point in releasing our forces in their behalf. They must themselves instigate the attempt to gain their freedom before we can go to their rescue.

Of course, we fully sympathize with your interest in the mechanical construction and motive power used to achieve the feats of apparent wizardry which mark our arrival in your material world. Even though we may, for some specific purpose, invite you for a ride, it will be impossible for you to ferret out our secret of propulsion, since you have rejected opportunities afforded you to become acquainted with laws governing these *higher forms* of energy. Such knowledge has been prostituted for illicit purposes of destruction, in the past.

Not until your world has dispensed with all need for destructive weapons and all desire to misuse the finer forces of this God-governed Universe, will you be permitted to experiment with ever-existent etheric energies holding magic possibilities for those qualified to employ them as intended by the Creator to whom they owe their existence.

We come now as Liberators but look forward to a more joyous mission, when we will mingle freely with you and gladly initiate you into many delights and privileges we possess. May we count on your cooperation in bringing that happy time very near? We hope so! My love and my blessings!

I AM ASHTAR

Commandant quadra sector, station Schare.

CHAPTER IV.

MY message concerns a number of erroneous claims being made by those who crave personal publicity. Any one who may attempt to invest us with powers of divination and announce themselves the recipients of information pertaining to the private affairs of individuals (unless they apply specifically to serious national or international matters) are guilty of falsification. Only insofar as they affect our plans (which must of necessity depend to a considerable extent on the understanding and cooperation of dwellers on your planet) will we pay any attention to your own purely personal problems by prying into the future for answers to your queries.

Our interest lies in two directions: Providing the facilities (unknown to your inhabitants) to prevent a wanton waste of life through the reckless employment of inconceivably powerful forces for destructive purposes . . . forces intended for constructive and creative purposes *only!* And, with our better comprehension of the principles involved both in producing and directing such intensive energies, to transmit (at the appointed time) to those proven trustworthy, the knowledge of a practical nature which we possess in regard to these forces. At present, anything we might add to the sum total of earthly achievement along scientific lines, would naturally be directed to warlike operations. We must *first* assist in the abolition of existing agencies bent on world domination BY FORCE! A planet populated by fear-driven slaves in the power of a mere handful of tyrannical (May I inquire what is the polite synonym for "bullies") rulers, would not even interest us!

Having held numerous consultations with the honorable gentlemen responsible for the founding of this country, our indignation has been aroused by the manner in which their noble visions of Freedom, Industry and Progress have lost the luster of their original inspiration and deteriorated into a dingy counterfeit of the original heroic model held before the eyes of the people. At that time much assistance of an amazing type was given at crucial moments. Inspiration and the courage and determination to follow these magnificent ideals, called forth overwhelming response from Watchers in Unseen Realms. Had they not been carrying forward God's Plan, depending on His guidance and His help, no such country as America would now exist!

I confine my remarks to this land for the obvious reason that it is here that a stand must be taken to rescue this precious and priceless IDEAL from extinction! Should this country succumb to the pressures now being brought to bear to submerge it in a World-wide flood of ANTI-GOD villainy, where might FREEDOM find a lodging place?

The combined forces of Space Men (assigned to canvass the entire global situation and submit a workable plan for the rescue of those being rapidly drawn into a tightening net of infamy) are united in what we believe to be the only means of handling this grave problem. Naturally, we do not propose to confine our efforts to this country, by any means. There are others in far greater need of immediate aid, being in many places, suffering hideous injustice and cruelty.

Before going further, I wish to make it crystal clear that we work at all times under the direct supervision of your future Ruler, the Christ.

NOW—What we ask you to do is to lend credence to our "reality" and our entirely *impersonal* desire to be of service! The sooner these two facts are accepted by people generally, the more quickly and easily shall we be able to achieve our goal and the fewer lives will be lost in the process. We are admonished to save *every soul* who will gladly adapt to the glorious transformation scheduled for the NEW AGE! Some may be removed from your planet to help for a time from planes invisible, as many thousands are now doing. I am referring to great many arrivals on the astral planes and a great many others, dating back to your beloved Washington, the immortal Lincoln and other men of their caliber.

We are submitting our plans to the HIGHEST COURT OF HEAVEN for approval and we look forward with confidence to your whole-hearted cooperation!

My Love! *A S H T A R*.

CHAPTER V.

ALL honor to all those who, through divinely inspired intuition, have grasped the true meaning of our mission who have not attributed our various manifestations to any base or selfish motives on our part.

Any attempt to acquire anything we find of value on the planet SHAN would be but the grossest act of robbery and utterly inexcusable, since your inhabitants as a whole possess at this time a supply pitifully inadequate to provide your population with the barest necessities for physical existence. We plan to *add* to your resources . . . not subtract!

It is not my purpose to call your attention to the *causes* for this ghastly reversal of all Universal Creative Laws designed to prevent any such dilemma. What very few of even your most advanced thinkers and philosophers appear to fully realize is the fact that innumerable purely material blessings *naturally* follow in the wake of a strict observance of these Universal Laws.

Even your own beloved Master, the Christ, did not *formulate* these Laws during his earthly tenure in a physical body. They had existed from the beginning of creation. They were a part of the creative process! They still are of the very essence of ALL creative process! Refuse to follow them and you *invite* destruction, as is self-evident in all we see of misery, want and degradation on your planet today.

The contrast between conditions prevailing on our own well-ordered planets and the chaotic disorder everywhere apparent as we observe life as now lived on the planet Shan, is painful in the extreme to contemplate.

On this account we do the more earnestly commend the heroic attempts by many enlightened mortals to rectify the blunders, as well as the purposely subversive activities of vast multitudes operating in direct opposition to the most obvious dictates of their own good judgment, did they but apply their mental machinery (however "rusty" it has become) to the discovery of the basic *causes* of your present difficulties.

Your planet was given a rare opportunity to learn the true and dependable Laws leading to progress along *all* lines of achievement . . . physical, mental and spiritual . . . when the One known to you as Jesus Christ was sent in human embodiment, not only to teach but to demonstrate in full sight of earth dwellers, the Beauty, the Efficacy and the Supreme Wisdom of compliance with those powerful Creative Laws enunciated by the Omnipotent Creator of All Things!

This advent of The Christ occurred at what seems to us a very short time ago and many of us watched with fascinated eyes and the most intense desire and hope, to see this Saviour of mankind accepted and acclaimed Ruler of the Planet Shan by unanimous consent!

Alas! The failure of all but a mere handful of people to catch even a fleeting glimpse of the sublime spiritual message He brought, which would have freed them from all *bondage* to material things . . . their complete BLINDNESS . . . filled our hearts with sorrowful despair of any possible chance for Shan to be saved from total destruction.

I say, we who watched from our posts of observation in space, lost all hope of ever seeing your planet rescued from the fate it had brought upon itself. And so our interest waned. Except for an occasional visit of compassionate scrutiny, we consigned your planet to oblivion as far as we, personally, were concerned.

Not so your Redeemer! He had made a sacred promise to those who believed and trusted Him implicitly. To them He said He would return in power and great glory, and this dark orb would be illumined in spite of all efforts of the Dark Ones to prevent it from happening.

We come now in full confidence that this promise is to be kept. We have been summoned to assist in the fulfilling of this promise. Knowing from long experience the manifold joys and satisfactions which will be yours when you are released from all those who hold you captive to their evil wills, we come with an excess of enthusiasm to lend our support to this crusade. Yet we hold ourselves subject at all times to the All-wise supervision of our Supreme Commander.

May we all band together in a divinely blessed fellowship and lend our utmost effort to serve well and faithfully until the GLORIOUS VICTORY IS WON and the planet Shan is at last a Shining Orb in the firmament of the heavens.

My Love! **A S H T A R**

NOTE . . . At the present time there need be no special effort made to communicate with us except at our special request. We ourselves will choose the time, place and person we desire to contact. However, it will be of immense assistance if you will maintain a feeling of friendly interest and confidence in us and, in your mind, hold a thought of welcome. Our forces find such an atmosphere well adapted to their work, as they need these

"Lighted Landing Fields" where they may pause for a moment or two and adapt themselves to the conditions and vibrations they must encounter in fulfilling their various assignments.

We know each one who is in sympathy with our mission and we would like *you* to know what a help it is to have these luminous avenues through which to reach the darker areas where much of our work must be carried on.

We are deeply grateful for your understanding and your welcome!

Ashtar

CHAPTER VI.

BY reason of the fast approaching climax in the age-old antipathy twixt two totally opposed basic Life Principles, it doth become necessary to provide more than human wisdom, strength and skill to overcome the heavy onslaught of misguided or purposely destructive forces.

Whether this assistance cometh in visible aircraft manned by powerful beings endowed with authority to use forces unknown to mortals, or whether the necessary aid be given in ways mysterious and intangible, of a surety men and women fulfilling the missions which brought them to earth at this time shall be given all they need to guarantee their success in carrying out their destined roles.

None may compute the wondrous patience and forbearance wherewith thy Heavenly Father hath borne with the frailties of human beings! None may even faintly surmise His disappointment at their refusal to accept His overtures of Forgiveness and Mercy! All which cometh to pass of a destructive nature be the result of *men's free* choice of the Pathway of Retrogression, which leadeth to oblivion as far as their residence on this planet be concerned.

> THESE RETROGRESSIVES CANNOT EXIST
> IN THE NEW WORLD NOW BEING
> CREATED!

A *failure* to bring about the establishing of this long-heralded "Kingdom of Heaven on earth" cannot be even remotely considered! Thy Master said, "My Kingdom is not of this world." Yea! But was it not also writ, "Behold, I make all things new?" "A new heaven and a new earth" wherein shall dwell righteousness! This be His promise! It be now in process of fulfillment!

Think ye the Creator, whom the most ignorant concede hath power to intelligently construct the globe ye now inhabit, be not able to re-construct it to conform with a program designed to give a regenerated human race the proper environment wherein to utilize newly apprehended forces requiring new conditions for their manifestation.

Ere the concluding contortions of terrestrial readjustments occur, ye may expect entirely unrelated, sporadic exhibitions by Nature, releasing long repressed accumulations of force sufficient to disrupt a mountain, flood a desert, sink a country or raise a continent. Not in a haphazard or irrational manner will these startling transpositions take place. They will follow a detailed plan of procedure whereby those areas best suited to the development of New Age projects will be spared or changed to render them fit for greater service to future inhabitants.

Any dissertation on future events must be received according to the knowledge and faith of the reader. A statement may be utter nonsense to thee today, yet a month hence appear in quite a different light. Let tolerance tincture thy criticism of aught which seemeth to verge on the fantastic. If ye are to be advised of miracles to be achieved during the coming months, then must ye admit to thy minds new concepts of Nature's part in this metamorphosis.

A plethora of cleverly concocted substitutes for Nature's originally perfect provision of foods containing all elements needful for man's sustenance have flooded thy markets. When correctly compounded by sincere scientists, we do not condemn their rightful use. Yet hath it deprived Nature of a responsibility she will again assume when changing conditions renew the impoverished soil upon which she hath been forced to depend for essential ingredients to instill life-giving and preserving elements into the matchless array of edibles she doth produce.

Be not fearful lest the earth be denuded of its fields of golden grain, its wealth of fruit-laden trees, its vineyards of luscious grapes, its expanses of greenest verdure producing all the vegetables one could desire. These and countless other bounteous provisions for the temporal needs of all God's little children of the earth shall thrive in the freshly vitalized ground which shall respond to Nature's alchemy.

> I HAVE SPOKEN! SO BE IT

Greetings From Your Friends of Station Share!

Would that I might personally greet each one of you openly avowed friends and express our appreciation of their kindly acceptance of the presence of those of us who come from "Outer Space" to aid the dwellers on the planet Shan!

However, since these friends now number so great a multitude and since "time" is of the essence of our present mission, we "Space Men" must confine our contacts to those occasions when something may be achieved which will in some way forward our objectives.

But I wish to make it clear to you that every new friend we acquire makes our mission a little easier and more effective.

It is not our purpose (as you have been advised) to "pounce down upon you" as it were, and intrude on your affairs in a thoroughly discourteous manner. Only in cases of unwarranted abuse of your newly discovered destructive powers will we feel justified in exercising our superior forces to circumvent their action, seeing it would jeopardize not only your own planet but many dwelling beyond the range of your vision. Other than this, our assistance will be supplementary.

When, through the dismissal of vagrant entities not entitled to the hospitality of your planet, we are able to mingle freely with you and give you our willing aid in re-vitalizing, beautifying and rendering your entire globe more tenable by progressive mortals . . . we can then express in practical and visible ways our respect and admiration for those willing and eager to lend a hand in the transformation which is surely coming to the planet Shan!

Our sincere interest, sympathy and love to our friends and those who soon will become our friends!

ASHTAR, Commandant
Vela quadra sector, Station Schare.

CHAPTER VII.

Greetings to Our Friends on the Planet Shan from Space Men Stationed at Headquarters on Our Base Schare!

THERE are a few suggestions I would like to make, in part to answer many inquiries by those serious in their wish to be of service in establishing the incoming "Kingdom of Heaven on Earth" and, therefore, desirous of giving us assistance in our initial efforts to awaken your people to the present peril.

While the cleansing process is unavoidable, as you well know, before a more perfect system can be evolved, there are many ways by which the discomforts and inconveniences of such a clearance of offensive debris can be lessened.

Whereas, in certain sections of the globe, nothing but a complete sweeping away of every vestige of ancient abominations and their residue will serve the purpose . . . there are countless instances where a determined effort by individuals, groups and organizations to raise their standards in conformity with well known principles of New Age living would obviate the necessity for such drastic measures.

Consider for a moment if you will, the *reasons* for this type of disastrous occurrences. Your own history furnishes any number of examples of corruption which led to the downfall of nations or their burial in the ocean depths. Has virtuous and humane conduct ever been known to wreck a civilization?

We are nearing the season when the people of this nation observe a day of Thanksgiving. It would appear to be an appropriate time to consider the blessings for which there is reason to be thankful. They consist of a vast array of material possessions which add to your comfort and pleasures in varying degrees. No country in the world has more abundant cause for gratitude to the Giver of all Good Gifts! And yet, observing the thought-streams ascending from the mass mind of humanity, we find a great preponderance of dissatisfaction discoloring even the prayers of the people! True gratitude, where may it be found?

You rise up in protest saying, "How can we give thanks for all the terrible things which are being brought to light . . . the treachery, dishonesty, deceit and disloyalty to all which is right and just? Tell us that!" Why ask so inane a question? No one is asking you to say you are thankful for things of that sort! But have you thought to thank your Heavenly Father that they *are* being brought to light? To thank Him you are being shown so clearly the evils which *must be abolished?*

Do you recall learning the multiplication table? What has that to do with world conditions? I will tell you! It has never been denied that five and five make ten. Or that five times ten equals fifty! These are facts accepted in every country under the sun. On other planets also. You start with one, then you build up by addition or multiplication to a hundred, a thousand, a million! And on up. My suggestion is that you start with "one" . . . yourself! Four of our Space Men will join you in thanking God for your freedom to think and act honorably, truthfully, justly, loyally. Other mortals will join you . . . and with each one there comes the added force from our side . . . fourfold! No doubt, you and many others have done this, not realizing quite how much it meant in the conflict now going on.

We have traversed the length and breadth of this and other lands. We have found multitudes of fine, upright, generous-minded people. We have taken account of every one of them. We have watched them at home, in business, at work, at play, in fortune, in misfortune, in peaceful times, when disaster strikes! At all times they are calm, resourceful, lending courage and strength to the weak and fearful! We know thousands upon thousands of such men, women and children. We thank God for them!

Were your whole world peopled with persons like them, what a Thanksgiving Day there would be!

Some think of us as "Destroyers!" Just sit down quietly for a few moments and think of all the things that make you anxious, afraid, unhappy, sorrowful! THESE ARE THE THINGS WE HAVE COME TO DESTROY! They have thrown everything out of balance, off their proper orbit! Yes, I mean physical things! The weather, the ocean tides, the air you breathe, the food you eat, the very earth on which you walk! They have affected all human relationships, business, government, commerce, society in general. They are the "intangibles" which permeate all existence and either destroy or create according to their character. (You know their names quite well!)

This coming Thanksgiving Day we from out of space join you in praising a beneficent Heavenly Father and His Beloved Son for every true, every beautiful creation of His which has not been distorted and rendered vicious by Man's misuse.

We join you in thanking Him that where you are caught in a trap and are not able to put into practice those good impulses and purposes you feel so strongly, He is sending mighty Forces to your rescue!

We join you in thanking Him that when this sad and distressful season of cleansing is over, we may confidently anticipate a joyous time of re-building, re-modeling, re-creating all things on this earth in perfect harmony and accord with the design and infinitely wise specifications of the Master Architect of the Universe!

To this glorious and sublime end we pledge our hearts, our minds and every power and skill we possess, till our sacred mission is completed!

We thank God our mutual success is assured and we shall see our Beloved Master, the Christ of God crowned King of Kings!

Unto Him be honor, praise and glory now and forevermore!

ASHTAR AND HIS ASSOCIATES
from Venus and neighboring planets in loving cooperation with all friends on the planet Shan.

A Simple Word of Warmest Greeting to All My Friends whom I Reach through this Contact Point: I join with you in honoring One who almost two millenniums ago, as you reckon time, humbled Himself and entered an earthly existence as an ordinary mortal. Needless to comment that I had known Him previous to this incarnation and had held Him in deepest reverence and adoration. How it was possible for any man, woman or child to become acquainted with Him and fail to give Him the warmest devotion of their hearts is a mystery too deep for me to fathom.

And so today, it is with joy in my own heart that I behold the ever widening array of those who truly worship Him, whatever their own particular form of religious observance may be.

Our Forces on Schare will join you with one accord as you endeavor to give expression to the honor due Him.

May you be granted a new and glorified vision of His majestic grandeur and absolute simplicity of speech and bearing and . . . Oh, that you might know the depth of His compassion for the erring children of the planet Shan!

To you who love Him, I can only say, "Did you but know Him as I do, you would love Him more . . . *MUCH MORE!*

To all my friends
"A Merry and a Holy Christmas!"
My Love!
(Signed) A S H T A R.

CHAPTER VII.

A NEW YEAR GREETING

*—to all who have accepted my friendship,
offered in a true spirit of fellowship!*

WHILE in a sense each morning marks the beginning of "a new day" . . . yet, as this last year has sounded the death knell of an era disastrous to the welfare and happiness of mankind in many ways, so the New Year just dawning promises an epoch of unparalleled enlightenment and opportunity for mankind to recoup his losses suffered through ignorance, or willful and deliberate substitution of man's base desires and destructive will for the Divine Will and Perfect Plan of God, his Creator!

Wearily have the days dragged by, while plots and counter plots complicated and multiplied man's unsolvable problems. We have watched with a horror impossible to repress, man's ineffectual attempts to extricate himself from the treacherous quicksands of deceptive "agreements" accepted in apparent good faith, only to be ruthlessly trampled under foot when their evil purpose has been achieved.

Why do we say the tide has now turned? Because all mankind . . . enslaved or still capable of recovering their lost heritage of freedom . . . begin to see for themselves the enormity of their folly in transgressing laws all-powerful to promote their personal progress and consequent possession of all they most earnestly need and desire!

When will Man cease his ridiculous attempts to obstruct the orderly processes of progressive development as set in motion at the commencement of his sojourn on the planet Shan? The answer is absurdly simple! When he acknowledges to himself that his puny brain and unruly impulses constitute no reliable guide to the acquisition of those tangible and intangible assets without which he cannot hope to escape a most terrifying fate! Might we, whom you have named "Space Men," share with you the actual, provable *facts* we have been able to discover by experiment and experience in taking precisely the opposite course of action to that followed by the majority of earth dwellers?

Not but what there have been numerous rash attempts made by incautious believers in Divine Intelligence, Wisdom and Creative Ingenuity to align their lives with this supreme triumvirate . . . but to what avail? Mankind in general would have none of them! Their fate is all too well known to you! Shall we share that fate? *NO!*

It is our avowed intention to acquaint you with the results obtained through the consistent and persistent use in *a constructive way* of the very forces you have used to *destroy everything* good and beautiful . . . and now insanely plan to employ to commit suicide on a global scale!

Our homes are built to provide comforts quite beyond your dreams of luxury unattainable! Their care is a delight, for there is no drudgery! Entertaining guests is robbed of all its problems save the pleasure of devising fresh plans for their enjoyment. (I might add they enter into all such plans with zest!)

All our educational facilities are entirely free, and so varied are the branches of study and practical application that no student has ever failed to find precisely the type of instruction best suited to his particular bent and ability.

Prisons, reform schools, institutes for the insane (yes, even hospitals) are unknown. They would be unoccupied.

Have these and innumerable other "wonders" come about through some sort of magic? By no means! We have worked them out! Where did we get our instructions? From the selfsame Source which is available to you.

I will tell you more should you care to know.

My Love!   *ASHTAR*.

CHAPTER IX.

ERE we proceed with other aspects of New Age Progress, we will spend a little time considering the necessary changes to be made in the habits of a majority of mortals, so that they may make the best possible use of new forces released for their benefit.

We will liken the physical body of Man to a plant which doth draw to itself and absorb into its growing organism the precise elements vital to its expanding life principle. If it doth fail to contact what it needeth in its quest for self-expression, it doth soon sicken and die.

As of the time of this writing (January, 1955) earth's atmospheric envelope be impregnated with many deleterious elements inimical to the health and development of any human body, particularly one delicately attuned to high vibrational frequencies. Such an one must be constantly safe-guarded against these infringing constituents of the very air they must breathe to sustain life. Not alone the air but the seldom recognized subversive thought streams, betimes well-nigh flood the mental atmosphere and drown out the more sensitive upward-reaching ten-drills of hope and faith.

To counteract these and other dangerous deterrents to Man's wholesome life both physical and spiritual, certain purifying processes be constantly employed by the Invisible Guardians of the planet, else would ye perish. Ye have observed what ye call an "electric storm" with its pyrotechnical display of lightning, and have noted the ensuing freshening of the atmosphere, making it a pleasure to draw in deep draughts of purified air. This be but one of countless artifices contrived to lessen the dangers lurking in the ether about thee. Other threats to thy health of body and mind (for they be woven together like the woof and warp of a fabric) be not so easily apprehended.

But this we would indelibly impress upon thy minds! A perfect provision hath been made for thine every need under any and all circumstances. Even in this transition period when ye do encounter many unaccustomed difficulties, ye have but to ask for Divine assistance to do the will of the Heavenly Father and, often in strange and unexpected ways, help will come.

Refuse to accept the ultimatum of Discouragement and defeat urged upon thee by evil forces rampant at this time. Pin thy faith to the redemptive forces sent of thy Heavenly Father to rescue thee from thy perilous position. As an airplane doth utilize the "fuel" provided to furnish the power it must have, that it may soar far above the sordid environment of a material world, so do thou avail thyself of the means provided for thy flight into the pure atmosphere of Divine replenishment.

Once thou hast contacted these currents of Cosmic Energy penetrating with ever increasing potency the finer, etheric Life Force all about thee, no heavy, clogging earth vibrations can hold thee in thralldom to disease of body, mind or spirit.

Until the Day of the Great Illumination, there will unavoidably be a struggle to attain and maintain at all times content and perfect attunement with this Divine Source of Life and Love Triumphant! Yet, herein doth lie thy freedom from the fretting exigencies arising from incessant friction twixt the fast receding customs and systems of a decadent and expiring age and that glorious New Age of unexplored marvels along every line of constructive and progressive effort.

Entirely new and fascinating possibilities beckon the dauntless explorer qualified to be the recipient of astounding new inspirations and powers ready and waiting to be bestowed upon him, after the necessary cleansing of thy planet be concluded, permitting the full influx of marvelous dynamics hitherto undreamed-of by the most imaginative of scientists.

GREETINGS FROM OUTER SPACE

A further word of information for those eager to hear of a state of development not yet reached by your most venturesome and fearless explorers into the vast universe of inexhaustible possibilities along every line of progressive evolution.

We would make it clear at the outset that we are not seeking to "convert" you to any formula of religious concept, other than the simplest precepts laid down by the Divine Master, the Christ of God. Many of these same principles were enunciated by inspired men, saints and seers, sent of God down through the ages. When the people of Shan refused to accept their teachings and put them into practice, they left your earth and transferred their efforts to more receptive minds and hearts on other planes and planets.

Whether you choose to accept my statement or not, it is a fact that there are no "closed doors" between those who temporarily reside on any plane or planet, unless through sheer stupidity, ignorance or absurd and unfounded *fear* you yourselves close and lock the door. Quite true, the "open doorway" must always be guarded by strong forces to prevent the entrance of unwelcome visitors. As you know, these guards are provided on request.

But to return to the more "practical" aspects of progressed living conditions as enjoyed by the citizens of Venus, and similarly enlightened planets:

As the entire environment and the atmosphere itself has become saturated with thoughts and emotional vibrations conducive to clear mental concepts and high ideals, you can easily understand that our problems of behavior are practically non-existent or, at least, reduced to a minimum. No one on any level of mortal existence (and we are mortals in a very real sense) enjoys being looked down upon by his fellows. Even a criminal aspires to be a sort of "*super*-criminal."

Thus it is that having established certain "codes of honor" in our everyday living and finding it a definitely *enjoyable* way of life, it seldom occurs to the youth of our planet to look for their pleasure in unprofitable pursuits. Actually they are too busy seeking to excel in their own chosen profession or avocation! Frequent "tests" are held . . . you would, perhaps, call them "Fairs" . . . where many exhibits are on display and trophies awarded for unusual skill, originality and dexterity gas demonstrated mechanically, artistically, mentally or along any line of constructive effort to reach a high and ever higher goal of perfection, with suitable recognition of each evidence of progress made, often works wonders with those inclined to lag behind. We keep a personal televised record of the progress of every student enrolled in our schools. Thus, they compete with their *own* past achievements, as well as with others in approximately the same category.

With what you term "The younger generation" reared in this manner, you will readily comprehend the way in which they are enabled to apply the principles and utilize the essential etheric properties contained in the super-charged magnetic orbit which surrounds our home planet. An absurd theory exists in the minds of some earth people we have observed that the type of existence we have attained must be slightly insipid and monotonous. Nothing could be farther from the truth! Our lives are fairly teeming with ever-expanding interest and activities! You have a trifling example of my meaning in the constant improvements made in your automobiles and household appliances. Even their method of propulsion is constantly subject to revision. Then, why doubt or wonder that, on a planet where war has long since been abolished and all diabolically destructive practices are unknown, we have evolved a system of Self-government which fosters individual initiative contributing to an Over-all Plan whereby each community forms a perfectly coordinating unit in an ever progressing planet of magnificent achievement and surpassing beauty. Our knowledge, our skill, our equipment and power to use it, all are at your service as you prove yourselves willing to learn and abide by Cosmic Laws which we obey.

In the Name of our beloved Commander-in-Chief, Jesus Christ, we bless you and give you our love!

ASHTAR

And His Men of Might!

CHAPTER X.

A WORD OF COUNSEL

—from One in Authority

MY word this day pertains to a subject of major importance: namely, the mission of what ye have erroneously called "Flying Saucers" and their occupants.

Our desire is to have them recognized as speedily as possible as direct emissaries from more advanced planets, coming at the behest of an Hierarchy governing this entire Universe; therefore, responsible for the continued existence of the more worthy specimens of the human race living on the planet Shan. (The Earth)

By reason of gross stupidity and ignorance of their superior powers, men have cast a pall of doubt and distrust about this entire controversy over the reality and purpose of these Men from Outer Space.

Since they be not subject to the whims of any who would capture, imprison and condemn them to torture in a vain attempt to force them to divulge their secret source of power, they cannot and will not be balked in their mission.

Ashtar will reveal further details of their heaven-appointed mission to mankind at his discretion. I Have Spoken!

AMEN!   SO BE IT!

GREETINGS FROM ASHTAR AND HIS FLYING LEGIONS!

Before writing a short resume of what we have to accomplish within a very short time, I wish to make doubly sure that everyone reading my statements shall thoroughly understand and accept my sworn affidavit that we "Space Men" have nothing—ABSOLUTELY NOTHING—to gain personally by this tedious and difficult task to which we have dedicated ourselves for as long as it may take to bring it to a successful conclusion.

Our only reward will be the satisfaction anyone feels in achieving a praiseworthy goal. Perhaps I Should add, the supreme pleasure of knowing we have played honorably our role in the forthcoming illumination of this entire globe, that your Master may assume His Sovereignship over a world completely renovated and restored to its original beauty, and even more than that, as men comprehend their privileges in the New Regime we shall assist in bringing into operation.

Is it not to YOUR ADVANTAGE to accept our aid? To augment and amplify our efforts some very fine, brilliant men are doing this very thing! This gives us the incentive we need to continue our attempts to gain the confidence and cooperation of all persons of intelligence and integrity.

The method I am employing at the moment may merely arouse your curiosity. But we feel it will take the widest possible variety of manifestations to converge and provide proof sufficiently convincing to permit us to carry out our plans without devastating interference. Devastating *not to us* but to the very ones we are sent to rescue.

Much as we would like to tell you otherwise, Truth compels us to warn you the situation is serious!

BE LOGICAL! BE COURAGEOUS! Above all, obey one of Nature's most insistent laws—the Law of Self-Preservation!

WE ARE HERE TO HELP! Give us a hand, won't you?

My Love,

ASHTAR

CHAPTER XI.

A definite change has come over the minds and hearts of many people in this and, to a lesser extent, other countries. Where, heretofore they viewed the appear-ance of ourselves in our Space Ships in the light of a curious phenomenon to be regarded with suspicion or shrugged off as irrelevant to current affairs, they are now seriously weighing our possible involvement in any coming conflict.

I am taking this means to advise you that most assuredly we shall intervene to protect this or any country on the planet Shan which places its trust in God Almighty and His Son who is His personal representative on this globe.

We have been asked to explain the type of cooperation we ask of you. The following suggestions may furnish a clue to our needs. Others will occur to you as you ponder upon the situation in your locality.

Acquire as much information as possible from all reliable sources, refusing to give credence to any doubts cast upon our sincerity and our ability to carry out orders we receive from our Commander-in-Chief.

Without being obtrusively insistent, pass on such information through every channel open to you. It is imperative that the public be alerted to our presence and its purpose. We might remark that treating it as "news" rather than placing it in a religious category would avoid disapproval in some quarters.

Use the telephone, private correspondence and casual conversations with friends, or even strangers, to promote a wholesome interest in the subject . . . tactfully leaving the impression that to deny our existence or doubt our friendly purpose is out of date.

Encourage the forming of space clubs or small groups to meet at stated intervals for discussion of the latest news available.

Stress the fact that our first urgent objective must be the removal of the causes necessitating illegitimate use of newly apprehended forces capable of completely disintegrating this planet and doing irreparable damage to *all forms* of living substance in close proximity thereto. We know the extremity reached in the downward course of power-crazed potentates! Under no other circumstances would we have been entreated to undertake our present mission or empowered to intervene and prevent the extermination of the inhabitants of Shan.

As the opportunity occurs, let your friends know we do not come as adventurers seeking excitement, nor as scientists in quest of fresh knowledge! What could we learn in your laboratories with their passé equipment, or what satisfaction find in the hurly-burly of senseless clashes in mental or physical arenas of action?

Perhaps it would be well to again emphasize the fact that your inmost thoughts and desires, as well as your acts, create either a very real barrier, or point of contact, according as you reject our way of life (based on the true Christ Principles) or harmonize with our concept of constructive and progressive living. We have passed through a long and tedious process of re-appraisal and re-evaluation of all Life has to offer in the final analysis, since first we were favored with wise and patient Teachers from "Outer Space."

What they did for us ages ago, we now offer to do for you! It is against every tenet in our code of honor to attempt to force you to accept our services in the capacity of Teachers. Yet this I can promise in all sincerity! Should our offer of genuine, practical assistance be welcome and the necessary preliminary steps be taken, we can and will joyfully pass on to you the knowledge we possess. Not only will we do this, but we will "loan" you many of our most expert and experienced teachers in every branch of art and industry to initiate you into the secrets we have tried out and proven one hundred percent effective in creating a world of incredible beauty and endless delight.

Until you have attained some reasonable concept of such a planet and such a life, I fear it would be unwise to extend to you an invitation to visit us in my home on Venus!

My Love!
ASHTAR

CHAPTER XII.

A LETTER TO YOU FROM SCHARE!

WE will continue our description of life on Venus, as a fitting prelude to our well earned privilege of serving in our present capacity . . . not technically designated as "teachers" but more in the role of "elder brothers," guiding, encouraging and commending any forward step, as our comrades of earth fall into line with our steady march toward our goal . . . the acceptance of our Beloved Commander-in-Chief, Jesus Christ, as Ruler of Shan (planet earth)! Until he mounts his rightful throne of Power and Glory, and is accepted by mankind in a true spirit of loyalty and devotion, we are bound by our sacred word of honor to serve in any way which will speed that denouement.

Let us, then, proceed to our task of enlightening our friends on Shan as to some aspects of our accustomed mode of "home life," which has afforded us a maximum of physical delight (my scribe questions that term) but we *do* enjoy the sensory pleasures which you fear lost as you make the transition into what you have named the "Fourth Dimension." True, it takes a little preparation to enter into this higher vibrational environment and participate to the fullest extent in the rare privileges which are ours. However, I assure you without equivocation our joy in the satisfying of every desire (since we have learned the secret of desiring only what is for our highest good) goes so far beyond anything you have experienced in your present earth-life that we are at a loss to know how to employ phrases strong enough to make it real to you!

When you "hear" the full, complete harmony of a celestial orchestra or the crystal-clear tones of a heart-stirring melody sung by one you regard as angelic . . . when a fragrance of unforgettable sweetness is wafted to you from you know not where . . . when a mental vision is reflected from some entrancing beauty spot, perhaps on Venus itself .. . when there surges through your entire being ecstasy which sets your heart aglow with love for every creature, for every growing thing from tiniest blossom to towering monarch of the forest, for every mortal who worships the great Creator . . . when you enjoy the full flavor of a delectable contribution to your daily repast direct from Nature's matchless storehouse of edibles (unspoiled by man's tampering processes) . . . have you not had a tantalizing foretaste of the "sensory pleasures" which many earth people imagine they must forego upon leaving their earth home which has yielded them all too scanty a portion of genuine pleasure?

Yet it is an undeniable fact that we retain, in amplified, intensified form suited to our more sensitized capacity for enjoyment, all you have found truly pleasurable in your "material existence" as you call it. We *hear* and are especially susceptible to *aromas* . . . though we have none offensive to our sensitive nostrils. We have *clarity* of vision, extending to realms hidden from your eyes, no matter how expert your oculist may be! Our sense of touch is delicately adjusted to objects cast in a more etheric mold than those you encounter, and more easily shattered. In fact, they may be altered or even obliterated by the power of thought alone (which might be considered a desirable achievement in the case of decrepit bits of furnishings I have observed, especially in what you name your "attics"?)

Please! I have the greatest possible respect and admiration for anyone who makes the best of their possessions however crude . . . but I was thinking of what you often refer to as "trash" kept about for no good reason. I heartily concur in "C. N.'s" advice to "streamline your possessions."

I have not touched upon the more spiritual aspects of our lives, which to us are precious beyond all else.

Our lives abound in an ever-expanding appreciation of blessings accruing from a free expression of our highest aspirations. We shall try to take you further into our confidence and our plans for your happiness when next we chat with you. Until then, my love and my warmest gratitude for your assurances of your confidence and affection, received by mail and via "wireless!" Thank you and God bless you!

ASHTAR

CHAPTER XIII.

AN EASTER MESSAGE FROM OUR MASTER

UNTO each of thee I address these words of earthly usage, that they may be read and understood by thy conscious thinking processes, limited by previous thought patterns strongly etched on thy brain, which be the physical instrument wherewith thou dost interpret My thoughts in conformity with thy willingness to accept Divine Truth in its purity of concept.

At this culminating period of intense effort on the part of *all* Light Forces to enter every smallest opening in mortal minds and hearts with the illuminating power of Christ-Love, it be given Me, the Christ-of-God once manifesting in mortal form, to give every human being *some glimpse* of My glorified Being! Until the mass of mankind be brought to a point where they yearn exceedingly to *know Me* (or the spirit of Truth which motivates My every word and act) of what avail would be My manifestation in garb of flesh? Would it not be accredited by the majority of mankind to some absurd, theoretical fantasies invented by minds closed to inspired revelation of Truth?

Lo, ye do contradict thine own selves! One moment you pray for a visible demonstration of the reality of One sent into flesh nigh two thousand years agone, that thus thy faith may be justified. The next moment ye deride and scoff at anyone who tells thee of beings (*not* from highest heaven but from advanced planets more easily comprehensible to untutored, immature minds) sent of the Father to lead mankind to a partial understanding of the spiritual laws by which man may progress.

My words of Truth and Life have been discarded by the multitudes as "impractical," have been distorted, have been mouthed in "vain repetitions" until they have well-nigh lost their power to reach men's souls, have been relegated to the realm of childish fondness for pleasing tales, oft cast aside as they grow to maturity. Think these be fitting preparations for My manifestation in mortal guise?

Oh, my little children of earth, list not to those who prate of vast stores of knowledge to be acquired through years of arduous study of ponderous tomes designed to confuse thy minds and divert thee from the simple, direct pathway leading to true companionship with thy Master in thy daily thinking and living! *One Truth* lived each hour of every day in conscious attunement with thy Master and thy Heavenly Father doth bring Me closer to thee than endless hours of reasoning about this or that theory concerning Life and its purpose.

To see Me with thy physical eyes would be to thee a boon beyond price, and this shall not be denied thee . . . yet will ye hasten the time of its occurring if ye will but behold Me in My spirit manifestation walking by thy side wherever duty calleth thee, revealing unto thee through our close understanding in what wise ye may best fulfill the tasks allotted to thee ere ye embarked upon thy present earth span.

Many now reading My written words be here as "ambassadors" from far flung vistas of "outer space," having volunteered to endure the irritations of fleshly existence that they might in some wise aid in turning men's minds toward a Christly mode of living. Unto these consecrated ones I say, "Lo, I shall give unto thee, mayhap in a way ye be not expecting, a true vision of thy Master and His boundless love for thee!"

Wouldst thou choose to see Me clothed in radiance of glory so dazzling you could not approach Me in thine earthly habiliments? Or may I come unto thee in seamless robe of perfect understanding of thine own earthly circumstances and problems?

Choose thee the latter, I pray thee, and in due season thy faithful service, performed in My Name and by My Power, shall lead thee to the hour appointed by our Heavenly Father when thou shalt see thy Master face-to-face!

Lo, this shall be thine own "Easter Morning" of never-ending, joyous recognition of thine ever present Friend and Counselor,

THY PRINCE OF PEACE

ASHTAR SENDS AN EASTER GREETING

What could a mere "Space Man" add to our Master's Easter Message which would not detract from the beautiful simplicity of His words? We, who come as Messengers and Deliverers from the "powers of Darkness" now encompassing your planet, beseech you to heed the note of warning concealed in this Easter Message and "step up" all your own vibrations to a level where you can bear the radiance streaming from the *glorified* Cross, which is the symbol of our Risen Lord, forever freed from the *limitations* of earth life.

It was said of old, "When He shall appear, we shall be like Him for we shall see Him as He is!" I wish to assure you, this is literally true as we have proven, for as we visualized the Divine purity of His Life and Teachings, as we made our lives conform with that inspired vision, we reached a point in our understanding where we were able to "see Him," not only with our spiritual eyes but with the sensitized lenses of our physical eyes until now, I can tell you in all truthfulness, we enjoy the almost inconceivable privilege of entertaining Him on many occasions when He visits Venus!

Some of you may question this saying, "The Christ Spirit is indwelling in each of us!" This we gladly concede is true! And this Christ Spirit manifests in many guises on all planes and planets. The Spirit of Kindness, of Compassion, of Mercy, of Joy, of Beauty, of Love in all its multitudinous forms . . . all of these are reflections of the Christ Spirit which our Master so magnificently presented for our emulation during His sojourn on Shan (the earth).

Each mortal seeking to follow in His footsteps acts as a magnet to draw to earth those qualified to assist in restoring that perfection of both material and spiritual beauty it originally possessed in the Mind of the Creator! It is our great privilege to aid in this restoration under the direction of our Master and yours, Jesus the Christ!

A glorious Easter to you in which we shall share, with all the hosts of heaven rejoicing at your response to the Call . . . "Come up higher!"

My Love,

ASHTAR

CHAPTER XIV.

WERE it possible for thee to see with thy physical eyes (or to retain in thy physical brain the memory of) scenes at this moment taking place on astral planes in close proximity to the earth plane, then would ye be relieved of much of thy burden of anxiety concerning the outcome of violent clashes now occurring within sight and sound of thine eyes and ears, as of thy conscious knowledge.

Soon thy superconscious mind will release to thee faint glimmerings of changes even now in preparation on the earth. Yea of a truth, they come into manifestation first upon the astral planes before materializing in earthly form through strange diversities of circumstance. Those most strenuously opposing their advent, do frequently act (quite unwittingly) as their strongest proponents. Seeing the frightful ravages wrought by devotees of diabolical dogmas, many turn away and apply themselves to plans for their eradication. In this effort they will receive superhuman assistance.

Following the demolition of destructive agencies, animate and inanimate, ye will concede the obvious need for a well implemented program devised to fire the imagination and arouse the aspirations of every member of the human family, in accord with their own individual ability to contribute to the Over-all Plan! Every faculty possessed by mortals may be fitted into the mosaic of New Age activities. In this way those formerly suffering frustration and defeat will feel a new surge of confidence in their competence to follow their clearly indicated aptitude for certain types of service in research, invention, mechanical skill, or whatever their talent may be, to a successful conclusion.

To this end hath it been ordained that many doors to knowledge hitherto barred to mortals, will be opened to those who through trials oft accounted unjust (and rightly so!) have, nevertheless, proven themselves to be worthy to receive the boon they long have sought. To them will be given the keys to mysteries long veiled from mortal eyes, awaiting the propitious time for their revealing.

Devious methods will be employed for the transmission of what be to many startling new facts regarding invisible forces, extremely powerful and yet (how wisely!) impossible to contact, or even apprehend from an intellectual standpoint, save by one elevated to a high level of spiritual awareness of the inviolable sanctity of any knowledge touching on energies emanating from Divinity Itself!

Not in any promiscuous and haphazard fashion will the requisite aids to the acquisition of such supernal knowledge be provided. Many factors will enter into the bestowal of such gifts, chief of which will be the *character* of the one in quest of any particular type of information, and his purpose. These qualifications may best be ascertained by a survey of his objectives and achievements in past incarnations. Such an inspection would necessarily be done by a very advanced mentor or specialist appointed for the task. The person whose past record be subjected to such scrutiny be not consulted or conscious of the procedure. We might interject the comment that many highly evolved men and women now on earth have undergone such an investigation and have been approved for admittance to the tutelage of adepts, awaiting only the moment of the world's emancipation from the domination of destructive forces to begin their collaborative work with their students. This active partnership between one in close touch with the material world and one in direct contact with supernal knowledge will be one of the major marvels of the New Age. The person privileged to enjoy such a partnership may not be conscious of such assistance but may attribute the sudden flashes of "inspiration" to intuition but will surely recognize it as coming from a source higher than their own mind.

However, it may be said in passing, that in almost every instance there will eventually evolve so close a companionship that it will be possible for the two co-workers to "visit" back and forth, from the Fourth to the Third Dimension at will, much to their mutual advantage and enjoyment!

AMEN! SO BE IT!

A FRIENDLY MESSAGE FROM ASHTAR

Another link has been forged between those residing upon your planet Shan and the galaxy of shining orbs (as you see them!) which compose the glittering firmament you see "above you." Actually, of course, it completely surrounds the globe whereon dwell those looking skyward at night-time from their particular section of the earth.

Oh, that all peoples could but realize how the encirclement by these illumined "stars" (no matter how far distant they may be as of earthly computation) provides the ultimate evidence that this "dark planet" may in time reach a similar stage of evolution, unless man himself decrees otherwise!

Could this fact be brought home to them, then would they accept a kindly word of counsel from the inhabitants of these and other progressed spheres and greatly profit by their proven knowledge of the beneficent action of universal Cosmic Laws, when correctly employed in a constructive manner.

Much has been written of late concerning certain visible contacts made by Space Men, or "Etherians," with inhabitants of Shan (the earth) residing in different areas of the planet. Their conversation is often alluded to as being carried on by "thought transference" or through the use of telepathy.

This brings to light a possibility given little consideration by those in quest of further information regarding any who have observed flying "unidentified objects" at incredible rates of speed. So impregnated have their minds become with thoughts of invasion by *enemy* forces (seen or unseen) that they reject the idea of a *peaceful* "invasion" or visitation by friendly neighbors wishing to courteously welcome them into the cooperative fraternity of constellations of celestial bodies peopled by those enjoying a type of intensely interesting existence impossible of attainment save by those who live in accord with Cosmic Law.

It is our desire to attract your attention and invite your confidence through visible manifestations of various kinds. However, do not for one moment conclude that this is our chief objective. God forbid!

Our revered and Beloved Jesus. the Christ, did "many mighty works" when He lived as a man among mortals, yet His real mission was to teach men the meaning of Life, both here and hereafter.

And so we rejoice that our vital mission to Shan is being recognized by many who meet and talk with us during the hours when their physical bodies are wrapped in slumber. The ideas, the truths, disclosed in these nocturnal conferences are stored in their. superconscious minds and our new friends later work them into the patterns of their daily lives.

As a matter of fact, it is of far more *practical* assistance in hastening the planet's delayed illumination, to change the "thought-currents" into the right channels, than it is for us to transmit knowledge of a scientific nature. Science perverted to *destructive* purposes, acts as a deadly menace!

Science directed into channels of dynamic activity which will lift the human race to a new, a higher type of existence in accord with its God-designed destiny, will bring into reality that Golden Age now dawning on the consciousness of all awakened souls. Our newly consummated contact with such souls is of profound significance to us and promises to play a major role in the emancipation of Shan from the domination of utterly subversive forces whether visible or invisible!

We pledge you our whole-hearted support in each and every constructive effort in every field of endeavor looking toward the illumination of your spirits, minds . . . yes, and the very earth on which your feet tread!

May our mission to Shan be blessed with a speedy success by the Father of us all and His Beloved Son, Jesus the Christ!

My love

ASHTAR

—speaking for a mighty army of Space Men now in active service.

CHAPTER XV.

ALTHOUGH the scientific discoveries and inventions of the New Age will cause endless amazement and discussion over the new methods introduced, a much more important phase will radically change all of man's relations with his fellowmen.

We speak of the "lectures" (if ye would so name them) which will be given in all parts of the world upon any subject pertinent to that particular section and the inhabitants thereof. These demonstrations of practical ways in which newly apprehended etheric forces may be utilized to lighten laborious tasks and increase the comfort and happiness of the so-called "common people" will be arranged by the leaders appointed. These special leaders will not be chosen by the people, since their duties will not be of a judiciary character. They will be persons of high intelligence and spiritual enlightenment, yet withal, keenly aware of the vital necessity for bringing these attributes into play in a realistic way, during the reconstruction period of the world's regeneration.

These leaders will make all arrangements for the addresses but they will not be the speakers. One of the very surprising incidents of the New Era will be the introduction of Teachers from the now "invisible" realms. These visiting instructors will be experts chosen for their intimate knowledge and experience along the various lines in which their audiences desire to excel. They will be garbed in accord with the customs of those who come to learn of them. They will speak their language. It will not be some "foreigner" intruding to instruct in the use of strange new implements and stranger modes of dress and behavior. It will be like one of their very own people pointing out to them better ways of managing their own affairs, that they may minimize and finally abolish evils long existent. Little by little, through their *own efforts*, in response to suggestions given, their entire mode of living will be elevated to a higher standard than they have ever known.

I speak not of deliberately retrogressive nations. They will no longer cumber the earth. Those of whom I speak are inherently honest and honorable members of the human race who have been repressed and retarded, not of their own volition but through forced subjection to men more powerful and aggressive but far less amenable to higher instruction and consequent progress. They will soon emerge from the apathy induced by domination to the point of slavery, and their minds once awakened will eagerly accept and put into actual practice the principles explained and new methods applicable to their daily tasks. By utilizing "moving pictures" (taken on other planets) demonstrating these improved techniques within the compass of their understanding, then patiently answering questions regarding the use of unfamiliar implements, they will readily respond and cooperate.

We use these downtrodden people to illustrate this system of teaching. By "importing" speakers from high planes and other planets to give detailed instructions on a multitude of different topics, fully illustrated, desired changes in customs and general behavior of the populace will be quickly achieved.

The very novelty of such an experience will lend interest and there will be a certain prestige attached to adopting the advice of these adepts from hitherto unknown sections of the Universe. Even the simplest of counsel will acquire fresh significance when given by so distinguished a coterie of speakers! This plan will augment and greatly simplify the work of those mortals who will be called upon to conduct classes for the enlightenment of willing but ignorant aspirants wishing to qualify for New Age Living.

None will be asked to sit in any dark and poorly ventilated room to meet these guests from realms long regarded as invisible. Nay, they will appear among ye as well attired as thyselves (sic—JBH) and ye will so welcome them, with unaffected cordiality!

This be a most pleasant occurrence to contemplate and it shall surely come to pass! It is plainly depicted on the Screen of Things-to-Come! Amen! So be it!

A WORD OF EXPLANATION
FROM ASHTAR!

A most gratifying change is now taking place in the general attitude of the people of Shan (the earth). No longer do great masses of the inhabitants of this and other countries, regard our super-powered airships as monstrosities threatening their safety of body and property but adopt a more sane and cooperative course of action, showing willingness to give us the benefits of a doubt as to our intentions.

We cannot but feel somewhat amused at times over the pride exhibited by those who have succeeded in registering undecipherable squeaks and whistling sounds on their poorly constructed receiving instruments! Were they familiar with the forces we employ in sending these signals (which are not, in most instances, intended to be translated into the language of any particular country) we could soon devise a method of communication satisfactory to everyone concerned. I speak of a mechanism. As the matter now stands, it is we who must acquaint ourselves with the curious combinations of sounds transmitting to your minds the ideas to be conveyed. These vary so completely in different sections of the globe as to present quite a problem to our men. Were you conversant with the art of thought transference, as we know and practice it, our friendly intercourse would lose much of its present difficulty and become a pleasing possibility. Our use of this type of "conversation" has been developed over uncounted ages of constant practice. When we employ your method of using appropriate *words* to convey our meaning, it is to us as tedious as if you had to spell aloud (or write) each word you wished to speak, which you would find quite tiresome . . . the latter often necessary in talking with the deaf. Thus (not intending any disrespect) we must perforce regard earth dwellers somewhat in the light of "deaf people" who must be reached through the medium of sight.

We ourselves have to a great extent dispensed with sound, so many noises to which you are accustomed (therefore do not seem annoying) are to our sensitized ears almost "deafening" as you would express it. You marvel that our Space Ships operate noiselessly; that we appear and disappear without the least sound, or at most a "swishing sound" caused by contact with your dense atmosphere.

Can you not understand we must *learn* to do what we have in mind, using the crude elements at your disposal, since you have little or no knowledge of the existence of forces we find so perfectly suited to our purposes? We fully realize how impossible it is for you to duplicate our accustomed modes of procedure in all the practical details of our ordinary daily lives, with your present limited "laboratory" of etheric essences suited only to the present atmospheric conditions surrounding your planet.

And so, my friends, we are forced to acquaint ourselves with *your* irksome limitations and adapt ourselves to *your* rather trying conditions, atmospherically and in many other ways, that we may be able to render the assistance asked of us in the present transition of your darkened planet into an orb of shining splendor!

That this transition must take place simultaneously on the material, the mental and the soul levels (irrespective of purely religious concepts), poses many seemingly insurmountable difficulties.

That which *cannot*, because of its very nature, or *will not*, by reason of man's free choice, be transmuted into a higher rate of vibration . . . must through "Natural Laws" (similar to the familiar Law of Gravitation) sink to a level disassociating it from that portion of the earth and its inhabitants capable of rising to a finer type of existence, compatible with the vastly accelerated (or "quickened" since it is more *alive*) condition in which you will soon find yourselves!

If you are able to visualize such a marvelously, joyously "revised edition" of your present doleful life in toto . . . then I greet you as future residents of the New World in a New Age!

My Love!

(Signed) ASHTAR

www.ingramcontent.com/pod-product-compliance
Lightning Source LLC
Chambersburg PA
CBHW051552010526
44118CB00022B/2680